THE
CALIFORNIA
DROUGHT

ECOLOGICAL **DISASTERS**

y Laura Perdew

Content Consultant
osué Medellín-Azuara
Senior Researcher
Center for Watershed Sciences
University of California, Davis

Essential Library

An Imprint of Abdo Publishing | abdopublishing.com

abdopublishing.com

Published by Abdo Publishing, a division of ABDO, PO Box 398166, Minneapolis, Minnesota 55439. Copyright © 2018 by Abdo Consulting Group, Inc. International copyrights reserved in all countries. No part of this book may be reproduced in any form without written permission from the publisher. Essential Library™ is a trademark and logo of Abdo Publishing.

Printed in the United States of America, North Mankato, Minnesota
042017
092017

Cover Photo: Jae C. Hong/AP Images
Interior Photos: Gregory Bull/AP Images, 4, 7, 42, 89, 99 (top left); Ryan Smith/US Geological Survey, 9; Don Bartletti/Los Angeles Times/Getty Images, 11; Walter Zeboski/AP Images, 12–13; Marcio Jose Sanchez/AP Images, 16–17, 98 (top right); Galyna Andrushko/Shutterstock Images, 18; Tom Grundy/ Shutterstock Images, 19; Kamil Petran/Shutterstock Images, 20, 98 (top right); William Campbell/Sygma/Getty Images, 23; Archive Photos/MPI/Getty Images, 24–25; Rich Pedroncelli/AP Images, 26, 58–59, 68–69, 99 (bottom right); Buyenlarge/Archive Photos/Getty Images, 27; Bettmann/Getty Images, 29; S.A. Smyth/Library of Congress/Corbis Historical/VCG/Getty Images, 30–31; Shutterstock Images, 35, 36, 40–41, 61, 63, 90–91, 97, 98 (bottom left), 99 (bottom left); iStockphoto, 45, 55, 74, 75, 76–77; Chris Carlson/AP Images, 46–47; Gosia Wozniacka/AP Images, 49; Paul Harris/Fairfax Media/Getty Images, 51, 98 (bottom right); Andriy Blokhin/Shutterstock Images, 52–53; Brett K. Snow/AP Images, 56–57; Brian Melley/AP Images, 64–65; Noaki Schwartz/AP Images, 67, 99 (top right); NASA/GSFC/LaRC/JPL-Caltech/MISR Team, 71; Irfan Khan/Allen J. Schaben/Los Angeles Times/Getty Images, 72; David McNew/ Getty Images News/Getty Images, 73; David Greitzer/Shutterstock Images, 78–79; Johan Larson/Shutterstock Images, 82–83; Damian Dovarganes/AP Images, 85; Lockie Currie/iStockphoto, 86–87; Reed Saxon/AP Images, 92–93; Gary Kavanagh/iStockphoto, 96

Editor: Arnold Ringstad
Series Designer: Laura Polzin

Publisher's Cataloging-in-Publication Data

Names: Perdew, Laura, author.
Title: The California drought / by Laura Perdew.
Description: Minneapolis, MN : Abdo Publishing, 2018. | Series: Ecological
    disasters | Includes bibliographical references and index.
Identifiers: LCCN 2016962231 | ISBN 9781532110207 (lib. bdg.) |
    ISBN 9781680788051 (ebook)
Subjects: LCSH: Droughts--California--Juvenile literature. | Water supply--
    California--Juvenile literature. | Ecological disturbances--Juvenile literature.
Classification: DDC 363.34--dc23
LC record available at http://lccn.loc.gov/2016962231

CONTENTS

Workers delivered bottled water to residents of the parched city of Okieville, California, in the summer of 2015.

ONE

EXTREME DROUGHT

In Okieville, California, in 2015, residents measured the water they used in drops, not gallons. Then, as the fourth year of extreme drought in the state continued, the town's wells went dry. Nothing came out of the taps except air or sand. The hillsides were parched and barren. Children played on dry soil where lawns once thrived. Layers of dust coated everything. Residents saved, rationed, recycled, and cherished every single drop of water. Nothing was wasted.

OKIEVILLE

In the 1930s, settlers from the dry Great Plains hoping to make a new start founded Okieville, located in California's Central Valley. Today it is a town of approximately 100 homes. They mostly belong to farmworkers and their families, who work in the

THE WATER QUEEN

As the number of dry wells in Tulare County rose, one woman was in charge of finding long-term solutions for residents. Denise England, water resources program manager for Tulare County, became known as the "Water Queen" as she directed state and federal funds to those most in need. The California Disaster Assistance Act had historically been used following emergencies such as floods and fires. In these events, the devastation is easily visible and understandable. The funds had never been applied to drought relief, so England's efforts were laying the groundwork for future drought responses. "You're trying to take things that make a lot of sense in flood or a fire and you're trying to apply it for drought," she said.[5] To begin immediate relief in Tulare County, England oversaw the installation of water tanks at private residences while at the same time seeking the viable long-term solutions residents needed.

surrounding fields on some of the nation's most productive farms. Maria Medina and her family live in Okieville, and their well went dry after more than four years of drought. "Okieville used to be such a pretty place. I had grass. Now I just have a poor dog chained up to a dead tree."[1] The Medinas are not alone. In rural Tulare County, where Okieville is located and groundwater is being pumped for agriculture, more than 1,700 wells were dry by September 2015.[2]

With no water coming out of the taps, some families in Okieville came together to run pipes or hoses into the wells of neighbors, sharing what little was left of the water in the aquifers. Many families were forced to fill buckets with the few drops that came out of hoses just to flush their toilets. Dealing with the water shortage became a tedious, time-consuming chore.

Other families began relying on state aid. Starting in 2014, California governor Jerry Brown allocated $3.7 billion for drought-relief programs.[3] Those who owned their homes were among the luckiest, because they qualified for a 2,500-gallon (9,464 L) tank filled weekly by water trucked in by the state government.[4] Renters weren't so lucky. Rental homes weren't eligible for the tanks because the tanks were

Okieville resident Tino Lozano used a hose to extract water from his nearly dry well.

considered a home improvement, and state funds could not be used for improvements for rental properties.

In addition to installing and filling water tanks, the state also paid for and delivered bottled drinking water, donated to food banks, provided public showers, and distributed funds to low-income families to help pay rising water bills. These efforts in the face of the California drought were unprecedented.

H2O TO GO

While the drought has caused hardships for many across California, one business has boomed: water delivery. In Nevada County, Garrett McInnis, owner of the company H2O to Go, was busier than ever delivering water to residents. Just as in Tulare County to the north, Nevada County saw a growing number of wells go dry. New customers called every day, wanting information about putting in a tank and water system and setting up water delivery. McInnis's business increased so much he bought three new delivery trucks.

WHAT IS DROUGHT?

It was clear in the daily lives of its residents that Tulare County was in a drought. Yet the technical definition of a drought is complicated. The simplest definition of a drought is a phenomenon that occurs when the water consumed by humans and nature exceeds the rate at which rain and other sources replenish it. It is a balance of supply and demand. A study in the 1980s found there were more than 150 other published definitions of *drought*, demonstrating how this phenomenon involves a wide array of complex and interrelated factors.[6] Adding to the complexity, droughts, unlike most other natural disasters, happen very slowly. This can make the start of a drought difficult to pinpoint.

US Geological Survey technicians collect data to characterize and classify droughts.

Defining *drought* is also a matter of context. What may be considered a drought in one area may be considered normal in another. As a result, *drought* can also be defined as an extended period of time over which less than average amounts of precipitation fall in a given area. Some definitions also describe *drought* as a water shortage, which is when a lack of water begins to negatively impact people, crops, and the environment.

DROUGHT MONITOR

The US Drought Monitor is a weekly-updated map of drought conditions across the nation and Puerto Rico. The map is created jointly by the National Oceanic and Atmospheric Administration, the US Department of Agriculture, and the National Drought Mitigation Center at the University of Nebraska–Lincoln. The monitor communicates drought conditions to the public, including policy makers in the government. The map shows drought conditions using several categories of drought intensity: abnormally dry, moderate drought, severe drought, extreme drought, and exceptional drought. In September 2016, the map of California indicated abnormally dry conditions or worse across the entire state, with the southern half experiencing extreme or exceptional conditions.

Scientists at the US Geological Survey have classified different types of droughts in an effort to better define the phenomena. Meteorological droughts are characterized by a lack of rain or other precipitation. An agricultural drought occurs when there is little to no soil moisture. Finally, a hydrological drought refers to times when the flow of streams and rivers is lowered and the levels of groundwater are reduced. The National Drought Mitigation Center lists two more types: socioeconomic and environmental droughts. Socioeconomic drought occurs when a lack of water affects the delivery of goods and services. Environmental drought refers to an extended period of a lack of moisture that begins to negatively impact ecosystems.

Determining when a drought ends is equally as complex and subject to context as defining *drought*. Some may claim a drought is over when reservoirs are full, while ranchers may make that claim only when their pastures have enough moisture to adequately support cattle. For California at large, which depends greatly on snow falling in the Cascade and Sierra Nevada mountain ranges, the drought will end only after years of snowfall have returned water storage to typical levels.

In California, and especially in Okieville, the varying definitions of *drought* provided little comfort. As the drought entered its fifth year in 2016, residents' situation was dire.[7] They couldn't wait years for water supplies to replenish. They needed long-term solutions, including public water systems. But even with public water, in Tulare County and across the state, water conservation was quickly becoming a part of everyday life. Forecasters considered whether the drought cycle was the new normal.

NEW PIPES

Slowly, the effects of projects funded by drought-relief aid trickled down to California residents in the form of long-term solutions. Water pipelines carried water to areas in need. In East Porterville, another town in Tulare County, more than 1,800 homes had either dry wells or contaminated water. As of August 2016, the first of hundreds of homes were connected to a sustainable water source through pipes laid from the neighboring town of Porterville. The East Porterville Water Supply Project will take place in several phases over several years. It is expected to connect close to 2,000 homes to the system.[8]

TWO

DROUGHT IN CONTEXT

H istorically speaking, drought in California is nothing new. Over the last few millennia, the region has experienced periods of extended drought. Yet scientists believe the one in California that began in 2012 may be the worst in 1,200 years.[1]

In the span of recorded climate history, California has experienced other significant statewide droughts, including

Reservoir levels dropped dramatically during the drought of 1976–1977.

ones over the periods of 1928–1934, 1976–1977, 1987–1992, and 2007–2009. By studying tree rings, paleoclimatologists can reconstruct drought and precipitation cycles going back centuries. Research shows mega-droughts that last years or even decades are part of the normal climate cycle of California and the surrounding region. Studies also revealed the years leading up to 2014 had the most severe moisture deficits in the last millennium.

High temperatures and low amounts of precipitation drove these deficits. As of late 2014, 60 percent of California was experiencing exceptional drought. This was partly because 2014 was the third-driest year on record, just behind 2013, the second driest.[2]

It was because of these extreme conditions that Governor Brown made a drought declaration in early 2014. In a public speech, Brown declared California was in a state of emergency as a result of the ongoing drought. He called on state officials to do what was necessary to make more water available. He also called on all Californians to begin voluntary water conservation to reduce consumption by 20 percent.[3]

DROUGHT SHAMING

As the drought in California wore on, many heeded Governor Brown's call to conserve. Others did not, continuing to water their lawns and wash their cars. With the help of social media, users publically called out these people on their use of water. This new phenomenon became known as drought shaming. Twitter users tweeted hashtags such as #DroughtShame or #DroughtShaming against those who wasted water. Some tweets also included pictures, videos, or even addresses. Celebrities were called out on their waste, too. It is unclear to what extent drought shaming helped curb wasteful behavior.

NATURAL CAUSES OF DROUGHT

The natural factors responsible for the drought in California were interrelated. To start, global climate change resulted in warmer temperatures, changing weather patterns. In the second half of the 1900s, average temperatures rose almost two degrees Fahrenheit (1.1°C) in California, with the southern half of the state experiencing the greatest changes. Urban areas experienced significant warming. In Los Angeles the average temperature rose from 62 to 66 degrees Fahrenheit (16.7 to 18.9°C) between 1878 and 2005.[4] Furthermore, California's weather was dominated by a high-pressure system. Low-pressure systems allow rain clouds to form when moist air rises and cools. High-pressure systems act like a boulder in a river, diverting storms with moisture around them. In these systems, air sinks and warms, leaving behind warm, dry weather that lasts for extended periods of time.

CALIFORNIA'S CLIMATE

California's climate is varied, from coastal to desert to mountain. The coastline of the state has a mild climate, with temperatures that vary little between night and day and between winter and summer. The Sacramento and San Joaquin Valleys, which account for a significant percentage of the state's agricultural production, receive 15 inches (38 cm) and less than 8 inches (20 cm) of rain annually, respectively. The southern and eastern parts of the state are deserts, with typical dry climates and warm temperatures. The mountains of California are quite different from the rest of the state, seeing great temperature fluctuations between winter and summer and receiving 50 inches (127 cm) of precipitation per year, much of it as snowfall.[7]

As a result of the high-pressure systems over California, there was less precipitation, resulting in a meteorological drought. On average, the state receives more than 200 million acre-feet of water per year. Half of this evaporates, is absorbed by plants, or flows into the ocean. The other half goes into California's developed water supply, managed by people.[5] By the end of August 2015, there was a five-year precipitation deficit, and between 2011 and 2014, rainfall amounts were down to 54 to 75 percent of normal.[6] Looking at it another way, regions across California were missing at least one

year's worth of rain. **As of May 2015, almost the entire state of California was experiencing extreme or exceptional drought, the two most severe categories.** The southern half of the state was missing close to two years of rain. The meteorological drought began to have hydrological consequences as the flow of streams and rivers decreased and water levels in lakes and reservoirs fell.

Another critical factor in California was the lack of snow, which can be more useful than rain because it acts as a natural storage facility, melts slowly over time, and is absorbed by the soil. Rain, on the other hand, often can't be absorbed quickly, and much of it drains into the ocean. California relies on snowpack for the water that refills reservoirs, drives hydroelectric power, irrigates farms, and provides drinking water. In fact, 30 percent of California's water

A 2014 rainstorm brought much-needed moisture to a dry, cracked reservoir in San Jose.

The Sierra Nevada range is a critical source of water for many Californians.

supply normally comes from the Sierra Nevada range. In March 2015, though, the snowpack there was a mere 5 percent of average. There was some relief in 2016, with the snowpack at 97 percent of average, yet observers remained cautiously optimistic.[8] It would take years of above-average precipitation to move out of drought conditions.

In addition to reduced snowpack, the warmer temperatures accelerated evapotranspiration. This means not only faster evaporation from soil and other surfaces but also increased plant transpiration, the process by which water leaves plants and evaporates into the atmosphere. The agricultural aspects of the drought were especially critical to California's $46 billion agricultural industry.[9] Many farmers across the state were unable to meet crop water needs.

THE ROLE OF CLIMATE CHANGE

The National Oceanic and Atmospheric Administration (NOAA) believes the pressure systems in California that have resulted in prolonged drought are due mainly to historical, cyclical weather patterns. In contrast, Stanford University researchers assert that climate change is at the root of these problems. Climate change is the increase in average temperatures caused by the emission of certain types of gases that trap heat in the atmosphere. These gases, known as greenhouse gases, are often released by human activity. Burning fossil fuels is responsible for a large share of these emissions. While Stanford, NOAA, and nearly all climate scientists agree climate change is being driven by human influence, not all of them believe these changes are ultimately responsible for the droughts. All researchers agree, though, that increased temperatures have made the drought more severe than it otherwise might be.

During the drought, California initiated a plan to address climate change that includes reducing greenhouse gas emissions to 40 percent of 1990 levels by the year 2030. The comprehensive plan also includes increasing the use of renewable energy by 50 percent, reducing gasoline use in

MEASURING SNOWPACK

The amount of snowpack in California's mountains is critical to the state's water supplies. During the winter months, scientists regularly go into the mountains to collect and record snowpack data. Specifically, they measure snow water content, which is how much water is in the snow and how much liquid water the melting snow will provide. Scientists also use satellites to get a more precise picture of the snowpack and the area the snow covers. All of the data together allows scientists to forecast water supplies, which in turn can help guide resource management in an effort to meet water demands.

Though nearly all scientists agree that greenhouse gas emissions are causing climate change, they disagree about climate change's relationship with ongoing droughts.

cars by 50 percent, doubling energy savings in existing buildings, and more.[10] These steps are aimed at halting long-term warming trends. But the more immediate, pressing issue for California is how to meet water demand during times of drought and into the future.

GRAY WATER SYSTEMS

A gray water system collects water drained from showers, washing machines, and the like so it can be reused. Prior to the drought in California, few people were interested in these systems, which were thought to represent extreme water conservation. At the height of the drought, however, companies that install such systems couldn't keep up with demand. While the systems can be expensive and complicated, they allow residents to maintain gardens, landscaping, and lawns.

PALEOCLIMATOLOGY

Paleoclimatologists study climate throughout history. One method they use to do this is studying tree rings, using core samples or cross sections of very old trees. When scientists look at the rings of these trees, they look for variances in the width of the rings. In years when the trees are not stressed due to drought or other factors, the rings are wide and healthy, indicating normal growth and years of normal rainfall. Narrow rings, on the other hand, indicate little growth and dry conditions.

To get accurate information, scientists must look at more than one tree. In a process called cross dating, they examine sections from multiple trees in an area. By comparing these, they can verify the ring patterns match or overlap. This technique can also help scientists overcome issues caused by so-called absent rings. Sometimes, a ring may not appear uniformly all the way around a tree. In some sections, it may appear to be missing entirely. Cross dating allows researchers to concretely establish the actual historical growth in a forest. They can also assign an actual calendar year to each ring and then compare those rings to the known climate data from that time.

During tree-ring studies, paleoclimatologists found California's climate history includes mega-droughts that last for decades or even centuries. Moreover, they discovered California's modern drought was more severe than any drought since the late 1500s.

Thomas Swetman of the University of Arizona is one of many scientists who analyze tree rings for clues about the past.

THREE

THE HUMAN FACTOR

W hile droughts have natural causes, the California drought was greatly influenced and aggravated by a complicated historical web of water rights, mismanagement, and overuse that dates back to the lawless mining days of the gold rush in the mid-1800s. Wealth seekers flocked to California to find their fortunes.

The human side of the California drought issue can be imagined as a glass of water with many straws in it, each straw pulling out water. Agriculture, urban areas, golf courses, industry, institutions, and more all have a straw in

Conflicts over water in California can in part be traced back to the gold rush that began in 1848.

OLD RELICS

As the waters in California's reservoirs receded, one reservoir revealed the remnants of a gold rush town that had been underwater since a dam was constructed decades earlier. When Folsom Lake, located in the foothills of the Sierra Nevada, reached a record low level, the old town of Mormon Island resurfaced. At its peak, the mining town had 2,500 residents, a school, and several hotels and saloons.[2] Much of the footprint of the town was visible after the water receded, though some parts remained submerged. Amateur archaeologists and curious visitors went to the site to see for themselves. They found stone foundations, pottery, rusty nails, and other remnants of a once-vibrant mining town.

the glass. None of them are getting the amount of water they want. Furthermore, the glass is not being refilled as fast as the water is being drawn out of it.

During the California drought, water allocation became a regular topic of discussion and argument. Overall, agriculture used 41 percent of California's water. Urban use was 10 percent, which included water to homes and drinking water.[1] The rest was allocated to keep streams and ecosystems, and the fish and wildlife that depended on them, healthy. Who got that water, how much of it, and when, was a matter of water rights that originated in the mid-1800s, originally established to meet the needs of mining camps during the gold rush.

To extract gold, miners needed large amounts of water. To meet this need, they constructed hundreds of miles of flumes and ditches to divert water, often working around the unclear laws governing water rights. Once the rush subsided and gold became more difficult to find, many miners turned to farming and used aquifers for irrigation. Others saw an opportunity, and they began buying up hundreds of thousands of acres of land bordering key rivers in the state despite laws limiting the

The water usage of San Francisco and California's other large cities ballooned rapidly as populations grew in the early 1900s.

amount of acreage one could own. The result was that a few people had enormous land holdings and water rights.

The guiding premise of California's complicated water rights is "first in time, first in right." Essentially, those who staked their claims to water or to land abutting water sources before 1914 have senior water rights, giving them first priority when it comes to water allocation. One of the most famous examples of this comes from San Francisco, whose mayor in 1902, James Phelan, hiked into the Sierra Nevada to stake a claim for the city along the Tuolumne River. He tacked a piece of paper with his claim to an oak tree more than 100 years ago. Because of this, San Francisco has water rights that are stronger than those of other cities in the state.

In 1914, the government created the State Water Commission of California. This new agency was the result of the Water Commission Act. Starting in December 1914, anyone wishing to appropriate water rights in the state had to apply to the commission. If the commission deemed there was adequate water, it issued a permit. All of the claims made after 1914 have junior rights, only getting water after those with senior rights have taken their fill. In times of drought, that means many junior rights holders don't get any water at all. In 1928, California added an amendment to the state constitution that required all water use to be reasonable and beneficial.

"Mother Nature didn't intend for 40 million people to live here."[3]
—*Kevin Starr, historian at the University of Southern California, 2015*

The laws governing water seemed, at first glance, to be a step toward reform and effective water management.

Unfortunately, they were unclear and lacked enforcement. In addition, the terms "reasonable and beneficial" were not clearly defined, and they rested completely on context and perspective. This resulted in widespread corruption as many worked around the laws to amass both land and water rights, leading to the rise of water elites. In California, these elite individuals and groups have the power to control where water flows in the state and the means to fight for these rights in court.

WATER INFRASTRUCTURE

In the early 1900s, local governments developed water systems to serve growing urban areas, including Los Angeles and San Francisco. Infrastructure projects began in earnest. One of the most famous projects, which also illustrates the power of the water elite, was the construction of the Los Angeles Aqueduct. At the beginning of the 1900s, Los Angeles was a relatively small city of approximately 200,000 people. The city's rich and powerful dreamed of new development. But the young city needed water. That's where William Mulholland and Fred Eaton came in. They sought to bring water from the Owens Valley, more than 200 miles (320 km) to the north. Together,

CALIFORNIA WATER WARS

When William Mulholland decided he wanted to build the Los Angeles Aqueduct, bringing water from the Owens Valley into the city, he ignited the first of many so-called water wars in California. The ranchers and farmers in the Owens Valley had plans of their own to develop an irrigation system. But Mulholland wanted water for Los Angeles, and he used his political clout and money—along with government corruption—to block the irrigation project and push through the approval of the aqueduct. Once the aqueduct was operational, residents of the Owens Valley saw the river draining and twice blew up parts of the aqueduct in protest. Ultimately, the Owens Valley shriveled, and other wars over water in California followed.

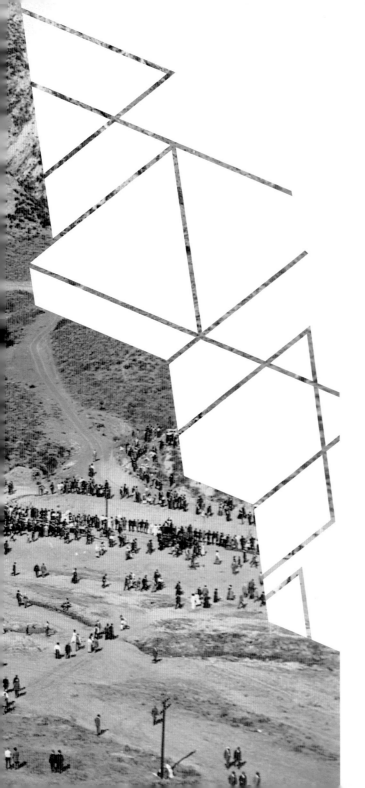

Mulholland and Eaton explored the valley for ten days in 1904. Ultimately, the city appropriated land and water rights in the Owens Valley, forcing out many of the 8,000 homesteaders and farmers who lived there. By 1913, the Los Angeles Aqueduct was complete, stretching 233 miles (375 km) to the growing city.[4] But plant life around the aqueduct began to die, and by 1924 the once vibrant, fertile landscape was a wasteland. Meanwhile, the population of Los Angeles expanded into the millions.

Other large infrastructure projects developed in the 1900s include the Central Valley Project, built in the 1930s by the federal government to deliver water to that productive agricultural valley. The Colorado River Aqueduct, completed in 1939, brings water to the southern part of the state. In the 1960s, California initiated the State Water Project to bring even more water to the

A celebration was held to celebrate the opening of the Los Angeles Aqueduct in 1913.

31

NEW GOLD RUSH

With water levels in California running at historic lows in the early 2000s, some residents returned to their state's roots: gold mining. Because the water isn't running as high or as fast as usual, these miners were able to access places in the waterways that were too dangerous to explore in the past. The state saw upticks in the amount of prospecting equipment sold and the amount of gold found. First-time miners, families, and experienced gold seekers all took advantage of the low rivers in the hope of finding treasure. Those who actually found flakes could sell their gold for $1,300 an ounce (28.3 g).[6]

Central Valley, San Francisco, and Los Angeles. Other state and federal projects, aqueducts, canals, dams, and reservoirs move water around the state to meet demand in different areas. Many of these projects not only move and store water, but also use the dams to generate hydroelectric power. While complex and costly, the system has allowed modern California to thrive.

GROWTH

In the 2000s, more straws are in the glass than ever before. In 1930, when the water infrastructure in the West was just developing, California's population was 5.6 million people. By 2014, more than 38 million people called the state home.[5] People have lived in California for at least 10,000 years, but never in those numbers, and never with such a great demand on the environment as is seen today.

Much of the state's water system was designed during a time that was geologically wetter than average. Water use estimates were based on those abnormal averages. As a result, California and other western states have greatly overestimated the amount of water available. Along the Colorado River, for example, seven states and Mexico have rights to use the water. In the 1920s, the states convened to negotiate how to divide the river water among them. They calculated what they believed to be the total river flow, allotted some water to be left in the river for the health of the ecosystem, then divided the rest among them. The division was based on an annual 5.4 trillion gallons (20.4 trillion L) of river water, but only 4 trillion gallons (15.1 trillion L) have been available each year on average since 2001.[7]

Some in California believe there is enough water to go around. The problem, they say, is mismanagement, over-allocation, and inefficiency, all of which have made the impact of the drought worse. Every player with a straw in the glass must innovatively rethink its water needs and be able to compromise, or the water supply may never keep up.

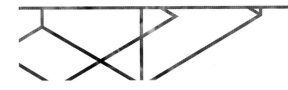

REDUCED HYDROELECTRIC POWER

One of the many reasons the West was settled, and populations were able to continue to grow, was the infrastructure engineering. Reservoirs played a large role, because they both store water and generate hydroelectric power. When the water levels in California's reservoirs dropped recently, little water was left behind the dams. Less water means less power. One facility in Southern California had its hydroelectric power generation drop 80 percent in 2015. Statewide, the loss of hydroelectric power was the worst in a decade, with the four years of drought cutting output by 36 percent.[8]

HYDROELECTRIC POWER

The drought in California isn't just about water. It's about power, too. The state has 287 hydroelectric plants, which typically generate 20 percent of the state's power.[9] In the first half of 2014, however, that amount dropped to 10 percent.[10]

These plants need water to generate power. Moving water, such as that flowing in rivers or streams or through dams, has kinetic energy. When harnessed, people can use this energy to create electricity. In the past, humans used waterwheels to harness the energy in moving water, often to run mills. In the modern era, dams are built to capture this energy.

When a dam is constructed on a river, the blocked water collects and forms an artificial lake, called a reservoir. Channels built into the dam can selectively allow water to flow into the structure. The water cascades through an intake and flows over a turbine, which causes the turbine to spin. The water's kinetic energy turns into the mechanical energy of the spinning turbine. The turbine is connected to a generator, a device that turns this mechanical energy into electricity. Power lines take the electricity to homes and businesses. The water, having run through the turbine, flows back into the river below the dam and continues downstream.

Shasta Dam, located on the Sacramento River in Northern California, is among the nation's tallest hydroelectric dams.

Reducing home water use is one important part of a comprehensive water conservation plan.

Chapter
FOUR

THE
URBAN SECTOR

F or most people in the United States, especially those in urban areas, water flows consistently through pipes and is delivered to their homes and businesses. When they turn on a tap, water comes out. Little thought may be put into the water's origin, the infrastructure that got it there, or how much water there is to go around. On January 17, 2014, however, when Governor Brown declared a drought state of emergency, people were forced to start thinking about these things and conserving. Among the measures in his declaration, Brown called for every resident in the state to voluntarily cut water consumption by 20 percent from 2013 usage levels.[1]

HOUSEHOLD WATER

People use water for drinking, cooking, flushing toilets, laundry, and other common activities. They also use it outdoors, watering lawns and gardens. Half of California's residential water goes to outdoor watering. In 2005, the state's per capita water use was 124 gallons (469 L) a day, more than twice the amount used in Pennsylvania, a much wetter state.[2]

This usage was part of the drought problem. For decades, people have flocked to California to take advantage of the lifestyle it affords. It had become an oasis in a semi-arid climate, full of beautifully landscaped homes and cities, lush lawns, pristine golf courses, fountains, and swimming pools. It was founded on the assumption there would always be cheap and abundant water made possible by engineering. Based on that, the development of both urban areas and new water supplies continued. The drought forced policy makers to change focus from the seemingly endless supply to demand. The mandate set down by Governor Brown to conserve was unprecedented. In 2015, Brown increased the water conservation goal: to use 25 percent less water than was used in 2013. Local agencies were left to determine how they would manage the governor's order and impose fines. Reducing outdoor watering and washing cars were high on the list of ways to conserve. Brown stated, "People should realize we are in a new era. The idea of your nice little green lawn getting watered every day, those days are past."[3] The new normal in California required a cultural shift and a change in habits.

Healthy, green lawns need a lot of water to stay green. To encourage people to shift their thinking about landscaping, utility companies offered incentives to residents who tore out their thirsty lawns and replaced them with native and drought-tolerant plants. Similarly, golf courses and cemeteries had to cut back on watering. The situation forced home gardeners to rethink their gardens as the drought limited what they could plant and water. Specifically, leafy greens such as spinach and arugula were good choices, as were peas and beans. Watering with used bathing water or unsalted cooking water from the home was also a way for gardeners to continue growing fruits and vegetables while conserving at the same time. Other residential conservation measures included rebates for residents who replaced older appliances and toilets with water-efficient ones.

And finally, in case the incentives didn't get people thinking, the governor also instructed water agencies to create new price structures to foster conservation. Under the new system, rates would be higher for heavy water users, rewarding the conservation-minded and punishing water wasters.

A MODEL CEMETERY

The Los Angeles area's Rose Hills Memorial Park is the largest cemetery in the United States. The 700-acre (283 ha) park is the resting place for 500,000 people. That's a lot of grass to keep green. Between maintaining the grounds and keeping the fountains going, the cemetery once used 293 million gallons (1.11 billion L) of water each year.[4] In August 2015, the cemetery began using only reclaimed water. The cemetery has one of the largest recycled water systems in the country. It serves as a model for water conservation.

Overall, Californians responded and water use dropped. The percentage of reduction varied by urban area and fluctuated by month, but the State Water Resources Control Board reported that between June 2015 and June 2016, the total statewide reduction was 23.9 percent, just shy of the governor's goal.[5]

Long Beach is leading the way for water conservation in California, saving approximately 5 billion gallons (18.9 billion L) of water per year from past levels of usage.[6]

EFFECTS ON PERSONAL HEALTH

Along with a cultural shift in how people view and use water in the state, the drought can also have an impact on human health. To start, the dryness it causes can affect air quality. Increased wildfires and dry soil send smoke and dust

Drought-resistant landscaping has become popular in areas that have been hit hardest by water restrictions.

Some residents of Okieville began praying for the return of water as the crisis worsened.

into the air, worsening respiratory problems. Doctors in California have seen increases in asthma, bronchitis, and allergies.

Among the other health concerns in California related to the drought was the resurgence of West Nile virus. The virus is transmitted by mosquitoes and causes an illness that can be fatal. The disease is spread to mosquitoes when they feed on infected birds; humans get the disease when an infected mosquito bites them. The number of cases in the state skyrocketed from 2010 to 2014, jumping from 111 to 801.[7] According to the California Department of Public Health, the drought's effects on West Nile were twofold. First, birds and mosquitoes migrated to urban areas in search of water, so more birds came in contact with one another and with mosquitoes. Second, because of the drought, less flowing water meant water remained stagnant, providing more places for mosquitoes to lay their eggs. To make matters worse, the warmer temperatures across the state lengthened mosquito season. Cases of valley fever, an infectious disease spread by soil fungi, also rose.

Prolonged drought also worsens mental health, especially for those working in agriculture or living in communities directly affected, such as Okieville. In Tulare County, doctors saw how the drought added stress and anxiety to people's

NOT ALLOWED TO SAVE

For a while, not everyone was on board with water conservation programs. In some neighborhoods, homeowners associations prevented residents from replacing their green lawns with drought-resistant plants. The expectation in these neighborhoods was that residents would maintain typical lawns. In the Los Angeles community of Brentwood, for example, applications for redesigned landscaping were turned down. In fact, it was suggested that if the residents wanted their yards to look better, they should paint their grass green. Finally, in January 2015, a state bill went into effect that stated homeowners associations were not allowed to prevent homeowners from growing drought-tolerant plants in place of grass.

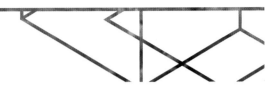

SAVING WATER THROUGH FOOD CHOICES

Another way some Californians conserved water was to consider their food choices. All food requires either direct or indirect water use—some more than others. For instance, raising cattle takes a lot of water, including drinking water for the cow, water for growing feed, and the water it takes to process the meat. In fact, it can take 4,000 gallons (15,100 L) of water to bring a pound (0.45 kg) of beef to a plate.[8] Beef is actually the worst water-use offender. Yet even lentils and garbanzo beans require hundreds of gallons of water per eight-ounce (227 g) serving. Chicken requires only 133 gallons (503 L) per eight ounces (227 g) of meat.[9]

lives. For many, their livelihoods were affected, resulting in a loss of income and the ability to provide for their families. People in the area worried about how to secure water for their households.

Questions about how to balance need and water use in California impacted all citizens in the state in some way. They also rekindled discussions about growth and population in the state. But the urban sector wasn't the only portion of society under scrutiny. Farmers and environmentalists also clamored for the precious little water available.

Dry conditions in Tulare County deeply affected the daily lives of many of the county's residents.

Chapter
FIVE

THE AGRICULTURAL SECTOR

Agriculture is at center stage of the water crisis in California. Without water, there is no food. In California, one-third of the state's land is devoted to agriculture. It is the leading agricultural state in the United States and has been for decades. Growers in California cultivate specialty crops such as almonds, olives, and artichokes. One in ten jobs in the state is tied to agriculture.[1]

The agriculture industry uses tremendous amounts of water in California.

EFFECTS ON FARMERS

Farmers were among those most intimately familiar with the dry conditions. Their livelihoods were at stake because of the lack of precipitation and resulting agricultural drought. Farmers lost income and were forced to let hundreds of acres of farmland sit idle. As of 2014, the agriculture industry in California lost $1.5 billion in revenue, representing 3 percent of the total production.[2] Considering the loss in water, this reduction was relatively small, thanks to the industry's capacity to adapt.

Many farmers have long relied on state water. But when Governor Brown announced water restrictions, farmers who rely on the state and federal aqueduct systems faced cutbacks. These were the first such cutbacks since 1977. In fact, some farmers saw an 80 percent drop in water allocation, and in the Central Valley, some farmers were cut off completely.[3]

To continue irrigating, growing crops, and making a living, many farmers turned to groundwater pumping. The laws allow for wells to be dug and drawn from so long as the farmer has the legal right to the land. Technology has also made it possible to tap into deeper sources than ever before. This is an expensive alternative, but those who could afford it had new wells dug to keep their farms alive. The investment was worth it, growers said, because they had already invested so much. Without water, everything would be lost. Others bought water from people with senior water

California produces 90 percent of the nation's tomatoes, 95 percent of its broccoli, and 99 percent of its almonds.[4]

Some farmers protested against government water cutbacks.

rights. Finally, some simply took land out of production or let orchards die. In 2014, growers took almost 500,000 acres (200,000 ha) of farmland out of production.[5]

RURAL SCHOOLS

In many rural areas, schools are the hub of the community, providing a meeting place for families. In the face of the drought, though, some rural California schools experienced large drops in enrollment as families moved away in search of work. In one district in the San Joaquin Valley, enrollment dropped 14 percent during the drought, and in Tulare County, one district lost more than 50 percent of its migrant student population.[8] Even more troubling for these schools was a loss of funding because state allocations of money are based on student enrollment. That forced schools to make cuts, and among the first things to go were arts programs and staff. Many residents in these small communities fear they will lose their schools altogether to the drought.

THE WORKERS

While California's farmers struggled to maintain their farms and ranches, field-workers and their families were also at the mercy of the weather. When farms produce less, less work is available. By late 2014, approximately 7,500 part- and full-time positions had disappeared.[6]

Cutbacks on farms started at the bottom, leaving poor field-workers the most vulnerable and struggling. Many looked for jobs hours away from their homes, traveling long distances each way for work. Others were simply out of work with few or no choices but to rely on food assistance. And while there were some improvements in the number of available farm jobs in some parts of California in 2015, other areas still reported hiring fewer workers than before the drought. Tulare County experienced a 19 percent drop in available jobs during the drought, leaving one in four families living below the poverty level.[7]

In some areas of the state, families were forced to move in order to look for work. Those who stayed lived under incredible stress, felt even by children who worried about having to wear dirty clothes to school, their friends moving away suddenly, or how their family would find enough money for bills. And while schools are oftentimes a haven for children, the effects of the drought were felt there, too. Enrollment fell considerably in many rural counties, and recess was often held indoors because of too much dust outside.

The fall in production during the drought also affected small-business owners in rural towns supported by agriculture. When people aren't making money in the fields, there's no money to spend at local businesses. Areas also saw more crime as a result of the financial strain. In the small town of Mendota, near Fresno, Mayor Robert Silva said, "The ordinary citizen here is going to be facing some of the most drastic situations that I've probably seen."[9]

WATER ALLOCATION

No matter how the allocation is counted, agriculture receives more water in California than any other application. For

FLOOD IRRIGATION

The practice of flood irrigation, which is literally flooding fields to water crops, came under great scrutiny during the drought. Conservationists point to more efficient methods of watering that can supply crops with the water they need while also saving water. These more efficient watering methods also lose less water to evaporation. Proponents of flood irrigation argue the loss to evaporation is minimal. Further, studies have shown farms with more efficient watering practices actually use more water because they can grow more crops. Also, on farms that use flood irrigation, the water not absorbed by plants eventually returns to the natural water system.

decades, the complicated and outdated laws governing water use in California encouraged farmers to pull more water than they needed, and federal subsidies likewise encouraged farmers to plant certain crops, many of which require a lot of water. Cotton is one of those thirsty crops, but farmers still received federal subsidies to grow it during the drought years. Many crops require much less water, but there aren't subsidies for those. Raising and feeding livestock also uses substantial amounts of water.

Farmers have grown nut crops more widely in California since 2010, even though they require comparatively more water than other

"[For] a grower, like myself, fourth generation like myself, who has so much emotion and so much of his passion tied up in dirt and production and making things grow, this is a heartbreaker."[10]

—Bill Diedrich, farmer, Fresno

Almonds grow in vast orchards in California.

crops. Plus, almond and pistachio trees are perennial, meaning they live on for several years and need water all year to survive. This eliminates the flexibility a farmer may have to rotate and water annual crops and adapt to seasonal changes in weather. The almond, especially, has come under extreme scrutiny. Critics estimate one almond requires one gallon (3.8 L) of water to grow and that almond growers utilize 10 percent of all of California's water.[11] On the other hand, almonds are one of the most profitable crops to grow and are seen as a good water investment for farmers.

OIL AND WATER

Oil and water don't usually go together, but during the drought, the Kern River Oil Field provided water to desperate farmers near Delano, California. The oil field produces 70,000 barrels of oil per day.[12] The drilling process also pulls up water. In fact, only one out of ten barrels of fluid pulled out of the oil field is actually oil. The rest is water. Once the fluid is pumped, the water and oil are separated. The water is then cleaned and conveyed via pipelines to reservoirs that supply farmers.

Policy makers have also debated irrigation methods. Flood irrigation, which allows water to flow along the ground, has been a long-standing method for getting water to crops. It can lead to significant losses due to evaporation, making it less efficient than drip or sprinkler systems, which deliver water more directly to plants. However, these more efficient systems can sometimes be much more expensive. Some stages of crop growth require more water than others, and limiting or cutting watering during the later stages could save much water. Precise climate and soil information afforded by improved sensors could also aid farmers in timing and allocating water to crops.

Even as drought conditions eased slightly in 2016, the entire agriculture industry continued to feel the effects. There

Irrigation methods became a major focus of farmers and lawmakers as the drought worsened.

were still 78,800 acres (31,900 ha) of fallow farmland, and the total predicted financial losses for the year were approximately $600 million.[13]

Some of the biggest water users are meat and dairy producers. Research suggests that if Americans cut meat out of their meals once a week, it would save the water equivalent of the flow of the Colorado River in a year.

Chapter SIX

THE ENVIRONMENT

J ust as people and farms rely on water, so does the environment. When areas don't receive enough water because of drought, whether natural or human-caused, the change affects ecosystems. In the debate over water allocation and water rights, environmentalists have become increasingly outspoken about protecting animal and plant species and their habitats.

Trees are among the many victims of California's drought.

WATER ECOSYSTEMS

Lower surface-water levels directly affect many habitats and the species that depend on them. Reduced water flow negatively impacts fish migration and breeding patterns, putting vulnerable species at risk. The Sacramento–San Joaquin Delta, where the Sacramento and San Joaquin Rivers meet and flow into San Francisco Bay, is one of California's critical estuaries. But due to the drought and overpumping, the delta ecosystem is in trouble. Among the species at risk is the delta smelt, which used to be one of the most common fish in those waters but is now listed as endangered. Courts have ordered restrictions to keep more water in inlets and rivers in an attempt to keep rivers at the levels the fish need.

In some areas, officials collected salmon in large nets to manually move them, worried the fish would not survive low river levels on their natural migration paths.

In the Klamath River farther north, the Chinook salmon, another endangered species, also needed extra water to aid its fall run. When drought conditions occurred in 2002, approximately 60,000 adult salmon died before they could return to their spawning grounds.[1] To prevent the situation from happening again, the US Bureau of Reclamation increased the water release from Trinity Reservoir in August 2015. Officials hoped the extra water would also flush out a disease that could become epidemic in the fish. Many other native fish in California are threatened by the drought, and environmentalists have scrambled to save them. Professor Emeritus Peter Moyle of the University of California, Davis, a leading expert on California's native fish, believes if conditions continue, the state could face a "major extinction event."[2] Eighteen fish species are at risk of extinction.[3]

Environmental actions have caused extreme controversy, to the extent that some politicians claimed the drought was caused by a government that cares more about fish than people. They maintained farmers were being starved of water even though conservation efforts were not working. One outspoken Republican said, "This is a drought that's been created by government, by their big supporters in the radical environmental groups."[4] In addition, some Republicans said

HATCHERIES

Salmon, steelhead, and delta smelt are among some of California's native fish that are in danger because of the drought. In 2014, due to low water levels and increasing temperatures, only 5 percent of the breeding salmon below Northern California's Shasta Dam survived. Due to concern for the species, conservation efforts were underway at the Livingston Stone National Fish Hatchery. The facility houses fish in all stages of development, from fertilized eggs to babies. It works to maintain a genetically diverse population of fish. In a typical year the hatchery spawns 120 fish, but in 2015 it raised that number to 300.[5]

that the drought response was being used as a way to hinder the development of the West and that water was being wasted. On the other side, Democrats and environmentalists believed the attack on environmental concerns was a means to deflect the conversation away from water conservation.

GROUNDWATER

Farmers who were not getting enough water from surface sources or federal systems during the drought turned to groundwater to feed crops. As the drought worsened, drillers could not keep up with the demand for new wells. And as aquifer levels dropped, drillers had to go even deeper to find water. Some wells were drilled as deep as 1,600 feet (490 m).[6] Because of California's laws, farmers can drill down as far as they want as long as it is below their property. By 2014, pumping groundwater met 60 percent of the water needs in California. This was up from 40 percent in years of normal precipitation.[7]

Some aquifers are recharged through surface runoff in wetter years. But much of the water in deeper aquifers collected over millions of years and was locked underground

ALGAL BLOOMS

Across California, bodies of water turned green during the drought. Algal blooms, which are large, harmful growths of algae, were responsible for the change. Due to the drought, less snowmelt and surface water were available to keep water temperatures cool, and the warmer water temperatures provided the perfect breeding ground for the algae. Authorities warned people to stay away and to keep pets away from the blooms, because the algae contains toxins that are harmful if ingested. In addition, when the blooms die off, oxygen levels in the water drop. This can lead to fish deaths and changes to the ecosystem.

NO BEES, NO FOOD

From giant sequoias to the smallest insects, the drought in California affected all species. The state's honeybees were no exception. In normal years of precipitation, California's hillsides are carpeted with wildflowers. In drought years they are not, which means a greatly diminished food source for bees. That means there are fewer bees to pollinate crops. Beekeepers saw a dramatic decrease in honey production as well, dropping from an average of 100 to 120 pounds (45–54 kg) to only 40 pounds (18 kg) per colony.[9] Beekeepers provided supplemental food for their bees, but even the best can't match nature's blend of nutrients. As a result, the bees in California were malnourished because of the drought.

because of geologic changes. During the drought, the pull from this limited supply was drastic.

The pace and degree of damage caused by taking water from aquifers was most apparent where the land began to sink. In some areas of the San Joaquin Valley, the subsidence occurred at a rate of two inches (5 cm) a month.[8] Not only does this put these areas at greater risk of flooding in the future, it also damages infrastructure. Pipes, roads, and bridges are all in danger of cracking and shifting, as is the California Aqueduct. The impact on the environment changes drainage patterns above ground. Below ground, once people pump the aquifers dry, they may collapse.

IMPACT ON ECOSYSTEMS

Drought affects even those organisms not living in water ecosystems. From the smallest insects to the largest mammals, all species in California experienced stress due to the prolonged drought. The dry conditions led to a loss of habitat and dwindling food sources. And due to the interconnected nature of ecosystems, changes in one aspect of an ecosystem impact everything else in it. A lack of water reduces plant growth, which translates into a smaller food supply for some animals. In California, some animals died, while others migrated. As the population of those animals dropped, the food supply for their predators dropped. The drought also reduced the plant cover that some animals use to hide from predators.

As water supplies shrank, more and more animals used the same water sources. The closeness increased the likelihood of diseases spreading. Among larger animals that migrated in search of more water and food, officials recorded more encounters with humans. Bears invaded the town of Three Rivers in the fall of 2015, in an effort to fatten up before hibernating. They strolled through town, knocked over garbage cans, scavenged high and low for acorns, and feasted on fruit trees.

The mountains the bears fled from are also home to the state's iconic sequoia trees. The drought killed millions of trees in the Sierra Nevada, and scientists were especially concerned about the giant sequoias, many of which are more than 1,000 years old and stand hundreds of feet tall. Researchers began climbing the trees and found they were under considerable stress due to a lack of water. Coastal redwoods were also at risk.

MIGRATORY BIRDS

In California's Central Valley, sandhill cranes return each fall from Canada. These birds are classified as a threatened species in California. The drought dramatically reduced habitat for all migratory birds, including the cranes. The valley provides a winter home for 60 percent of the world's remaining sandhill cranes, which number approximately 10,000.[10] Not only were wildlife refuges dried up, but fewer farmers used flood irrigation in response to the drought. This further diminished available wetlands for the birds. The result was that the birds crowded together in tighter spaces, making populations more vulnerable to disease and forcing them to compete more for scarce resources.

Across the state, experts estimated more than 30 million trees died by 2016 as a result of the drought.[11] The numbers weren't expected to improve, especially because weak, dehydrated trees are more susceptible to bark beetles. Once inside a tree, these insects are able to kill it. The high tree mortality suggests California's landscape will change significantly in the coming years.

"We can have both a healthy environment and economy—including agriculture. But if we continue to sacrifice environmental protections instead of investing in long-term water solutions, we will probably have neither."[12]

—Doug Obegi, environmental attorney, 2016

In places such as the town of Three Rivers, drought has driven dangerous wild animals into close contact with humans.

AQUIFERS

Aquifers are underground layers of rock that act as natural storage tanks for water. They consist of layers of sedimentary rock, such as sandstone. These rock layers are permeable, allowing water to pass through them as it seeps into the ground from snowmelt, rain, or other surface water. Major aquifers underlie much of the United States.

The aquifers are part of the water cycle, the process by which water evaporates, condenses into clouds, and falls as precipitation. They are recharged as gravity pulls surface water through the ground. Some of this water moves slowly, only a few centimeters in 100 years.

In other areas, underground water can move several feet every day.

The water in aquifers can remain there for centuries, and hydrologists believe some water underground today was trapped there more than 10,000 years ago. The oldest water ever discovered, located in a Canadian mine, was estimated to have first fallen as precipitation more than 1.5 billion years ago. NOAA estimates that 30 percent of all of Earth's liquid freshwater is stored in aquifers.[13]

Enormous aquifers sometimes underlie areas that are otherwise dry.

SEVEN

WILDFIRES

In a healthy forest, natural fires are often beneficial, moving through quickly and revitalizing the forest. But in forests filled with dead and dry trees, fires burn hotter and longer because of all the additional fuel, effectively killing everything in their paths. In such high-intensity fires, even healthy groups of trees don't stand a chance. These fires can threaten ecosystems and nearby human residents.

A NEW KIND OF FIRE

Fires are a natural part of many ecosystems, especially in California. Plants living there have evolved with fires and

Firefighters battled a huge blaze near Fresh Pond, California, in September 2014.

CAUSES OF WILDFIRES

Historically, lightning caused most wildfires. Lightning still causes some wildfires today, but humans start the majority of fires. Most human-caused fires are accidents. Campfires, smoking, burning trash, and fireworks can all start wildland fires. Children playing with matches have also started wildfires. A few fires in California have been the result of arson. In fact, a devastating fire in Lower Lake that wiped out much of the town's commercial district and burned 4,000 acres (1,600 ha) was started by a resident of a nearby town.[2] Police arrested the man, who faced multiple counts of arson for several fires.

are adapted to withstand them. Fires recycle nutrients that may be locked within dead leaves and stems. After a fire, new growth emerges from existing root systems and is fertilized by ash. Historically, fires that moved across California's landscape were smaller than those seen in the last century. They kept ecosystems healthy. But during the recent drought, millions of dead and stressed trees, a lack of moisture in the soil and vegetation, and rising temperatures have led to massive wildfires that have been larger, hotter, and more devastating than those in the past.

In 2016, California experienced its hottest summer on record. The higher temperatures and lack of moisture created situations in which vegetation dried out sooner in the spring and stayed dry later into the fall. Trees were stressed and dying under these conditions. By September 2016, only two-thirds of the way through the year, almost 500,000 acres (200,000 ha) had burned in the state. This amount was higher than the totals in either of the previous two years. A study funded by the California Energy Commission and NOAA predicts that by the 2100s, California will see a 15 to 70 percent increase in the acreage burned by fires each year, compared with the 1961–1990 annual average.[1]

Headlines from California since the drought began have included statements about destructive fires. They came one right after another, with each fire seemingly outdoing the last. California's wildfire season had historically been between June and October, but in the wake of the drought, fires were able to occur year-round. Officials warned residents that this might be the new normal.

ENVIRONMENTAL COST

After fire has gobbled up everything in its path, it leaves behind blackened landscape, charred trees, and ash. Fires destabilize and even destroy ecosystems. Instead of being revitalized in the fire, plants and trees are killed altogether, and it takes longer for plant life to reestablish itself.

Massive fires can also lead to landslides. Without vegetation to hold soil in place, the soil becomes unstable and susceptible to flash flooding and mudslides. When this happens, debris and sediment wind up in watersheds, contaminating water supplies.

Air quality in California was also compromised as a result of the drought. Because of the size and frequency of fires

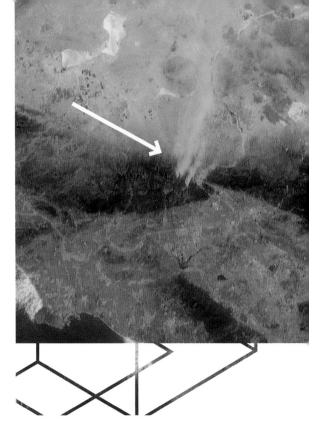

THE BLUE CUT FIRE

One of the dozens of fires in California in summer 2016 was the Blue Cut fire. In August of that year, near Cajon Pass in Southern California, a fire ignited and quickly became enormous. Within a week, it became one of the most destructive fires in California's history. As the fire raged on, authorities evacuated many neighborhoods. Local, state, and interstate roads were closed, and railroad lines were shut down. More than 2,000 firefighters from across the United States helped battle the blaze. No lives were lost, but the fire burned nearly 37,000 acres (15,000 ha) and destroyed 105 homes.[3]

in the state, researchers at the Yale School of Forestry and Environmental Studies predicted air quality would worsen. Smoke and soot irritate lungs. Because the particles are so small, one-thirtieth the thickness of a human hair, they can lodge deep in the lungs and eventually move into the bloodstream, poisoning people. Those near a fire aren't the only ones affected. Air pollution from fires can travel thousands of miles, posing health risks to large numbers of people.

ECONOMIC COSTS

The fires that burned across the state of California didn't limit themselves to forests and grasslands. Fueled by winds and dry conditions, they spread into inhabited areas, threatening homes and businesses. When that happened, officials sent out mandatory evacuation orders. Thousands of residents in California received such calls and were forced to pack up treasured belongings and flee the area. Oftentimes shelters were set up for evacuees. Some people turned to friends and families for a place to stay. Then they waited and watched the news, hoping to hear that the fire had spared their homes. The lucky ones were able to return home after evacuation orders

HISTORIC DINER DESTROYED

News reports of massive wildfires often cover the number of acres burned or show images of family homes destroyed in a fire's path. But businesses are also affected, as are historic sites. In 2016, the Blue Cut fire in San Bernardino County destroyed a diner that was a part of the history of old US Route 66. This famous highway ran from Illinois to California. The Summit Inn was originally opened in the early 1950s on a section of the highway that stretched between Los Angeles and Las Vegas, Nevada. It was a beloved stopping spot for travelers.

Wildfires can char the grasslands animals use for grazing.

Helicopters can pick up water in buckets, then drop it over raging wildfires.

Firebreaks are designed to reduce or remove flammable material from a fire's path.

were lifted. Others returned only to find a pile of smoldering rubble where their house once stood.

The state and federal governments also pay the price for fighting these fires. In 2015, the US Forest Service spent half its budget fighting wildfires across the West.[4] This money paid for equipment, vehicles, and firefighters. Workers on

"The conditions for fire are getting worse. There are longer fire seasons, and the fire seasons that are more extreme are happening more frequently."[5]

—*Mark Cochrane, fire ecologist at South Dakota State University*

the ground cut trenches and cleared brush to create firebreaks, attempting to keep fires from advancing. Many fires were also fought from the air, using helicopters to dump water and fire retardant on hard-to-reach areas. In 2014, the California Department of Forestry and Fire Protection spent more than $200 million on fighting fires.[6]

FIRE SUPPRESSION

Another factor contributing to California's wildfires is the history of fire suppression. In the early part of the 1900s, states began to actively fight fires for fear they might get out of control and spread. This approach, however, was shortsighted. Fires are a natural occurrence and play a significant role in maintaining the health of ecosystems. As a result of the firefighting, decades' worth of underbrush was allowed to build up instead of being burned in small, low-intensity fires. Over time, this littered the landscape with fuel for large, hot fires.

California firefighters often work in remote locations to combat the spread of devastating forest fires.

EIGHT

LIVING WITH THE NEW NORMAL

As the drought in California entered its fifth year in 2016, reservoir levels were dangerously low, agricultural fields lay fallow, wildfires were increasing in frequency, ecosystems were dying, and water use restrictions were still in place.

Water levels in Lake Shasta dropped dozens of feet, leaving houseboats on the lake crammed into its remaining surface area.

Californians were learning to live with the new normal. Yet people still needed water, and the question of how to provide it in the face of a potentially unending drought became increasingly pressing.

SHORT-TERM SOLUTIONS

For the short term, Governor Brown unveiled a $1 billion emergency-relief plan in 2015. At least $200 million of that was dedicated to funding projects focused on recycling and desalinating water.[1] Despite the dry conditions, a large part of the remaining money was marked for flood relief efforts. Brown warned that unpredictable changes in weather patterns bring the potential for extreme storms and flooding. This came after state and local governments had previously allocated millions of dollars for emergency food and water for residents. Urban areas were also conserving water and finding creative ways to use less of it. Farmers received less water from the federal system. And the state was stricter about imposing fines.

Fixing and updating the state's aging water infrastructure would also help save millions of gallons of water every year. As of 2015, California cities lost 15 percent of their water to leaks, breaks, and spills.[3] Because the drought did not seem to be showing signs of letting up, California and other states in the West began looking for more long-term, sustainable solutions.

LONG-TERM SOLUTIONS

To address its water issues, California turned to Australia's example. Australia not only has a climate similar to California, with deserts inland and a populated, more temperate coastline, but also has a similar system of water delivery. When Australia began experiencing the Big Dry—a ten-year drought that started in 2003—the response from farmers, politicians, and the public was similar to that in California. People were resistant to change and bickered over water allocation. As Australia's drought wore on, though, the country invested in conservation education and efficiency. It also reexamined age-old water-rights laws. Today Australia treats water as a commodity as opposed to a public resource, and people trade and conserve it. There are also new systems in place to track water levels and water use. Average daily use per person in Australia is 55 gallons (208 L) per day, compared to 105 gallons (397 L) per day in California.[4]

WATER FENCES

California high school freshman Steven McDowell wanted to develop a way to store water without placing a large tank in his yard. He realized that in his neighborhood, everyone had a fence or wall, and he wondered if anyone had ever thought to use them to capture rainwater from the roof and store it. In some states, there are regulations surrounding the capture and storage of rainwater, since this takes away water that would normally drain away for public usage. In California, it is permitted if the system's user follows government requirements. McDowell designed and built a model of his water fence idea for a science fair project. He calculated that an inch of rain falling on a 2,000-square-foot (186 sq m) roof would harvest 1,200 gallons (4,500 L) of water.[5] The water runs off the roof into a hollow fence, where it is stored. The water can then be used for gardens, lawns, or pools. McDowell won his science fair and other regional fairs. He also won numerous other awards, including an American Meteorological Society Certificate of Outstanding Achievement, and patented his idea.

In addition to revised water rights, home water-recycling systems, rooftop rain collectors, and high-efficiency appliances are now commonplace in Australia. In California, the number of residents and businesses using such methods has grown, but even in the face of the drought, they are not the norm. A complete cultural shift in how water is consumed in California is needed. Historically Californians believed water to be abundant and cheap for farming and thirsty, growing urban areas. In many areas of California, arid or semi-arid valleys became lush communities with pools, golf courses, and productive agricultural fields.

Part of this cultural shift will demand stronger regulation and more planning concerning development and growth in the state. The Coachella Valley east of Los Angeles,

Australia's lengthy drought left farm fields dry and dusty.

for example, is extremely dry, receiving only 3 to 4 inches (7.6 to 10.2 cm) of rain per year. Despite mounting water concerns, development there continues. The area's population is expected to grow from approximately 500,000 in 2015 to 812,000 in 2035.[6] The situation across the state is similar. The growth seems unsustainable at its current pace. In the Coachella Valley, officials have finally recognized that conservation and recycling efforts must be part of planning.

The Sustainable Groundwater Management Act (SGMA), passed by the state of California in 2014, calls for the establishment of local agencies throughout the state to manage groundwater resources. Each agency is tasked with evaluating the conditions in its own area and developing plans to maintain the groundwater there. The overall aim of the

WATER PIPELINES

As California looked to meet its demand for water, the state considered purchasing water from Alaska. The original idea to bring water 1,400 miles (2,250 km) from Alaska to California was considered in the 1980s.[7] That idea called for a massive pipeline. Due to the huge engineering costs, the pipeline was never built. In 2015, thoughts turned once again to Alaska, and a company there proposed moving the water via a tanker ship. Various water districts considered the idea, but costs for infrastructure, shipping, and the water itself would be steep.

Saudi Arabia relies on desalination to meet 70 percent of its water demand.[8]

SGMA is to provide long-term sustainability for groundwater in California.

TECHNOLOGY

Two of the most promising technological innovations for California are desalination plants and recycling systems. California is a coastal state, with hundreds of miles abutting the Pacific Ocean, but the ocean's salty water is undrinkable. Scientists have worked to come up with cost-effective ways to desalinate the water to make it more useful. And while desalination plants successfully deliver quality water to some citizens in California and in other parts of the world, they are also controversial because of their energy demands. They provide clean water, but they also require a lot of energy, which can lead to increased greenhouse gas emissions. The plants can be expensive to operate, too. There are also challenges around the disposal of brine, the highly salty water that is one of the waste products of desalination.

Another long-term solution has been to capture wastewater for recycling. Many places capture and treat wastewater, then return it to the system for irrigation or to replenish aquifers. San Diego has such a project in the works.

It is designed to treat water that's already in the system and put it back in reservoirs. The plant, built by the Pure Water San Diego program, will send the used water through three cleaning steps in an effort to make it as pure as possible. By 2035, the city aims to provide one-third of its water through such local systems, creating a sustainable water supply for the future.[9]

Others believe part of the solution lies in agriculture, and that much of the recycled water could be used for crops. Near Monterey Bay, a wastewater plant recycles seven million gallons (27 million L) a day and sends it out to farmers. Some have called the system "showers to flowers."[10] It is an effort to preserve the farms in the nearby Pajaro Valley, where farmers grow berries and vegetables. When farmers are able to use recycled water, they aren't forced to pump groundwater to grow their crops.

Farmers have also switched to crops that require less water. Vineyards, for example, require 25 percent less water than citrus groves. During the drought, the number of vineyards increased, and the number of citrus groves decreased. Avocados are also thirsty crops, and growers took many of

LOW-TECH SOLUTIONS

The ongoing drought in California left the state considering any and all solutions to harness and conserve water. One that drew a great deal of scrutiny was the release of 96 million "shade balls" into the Los Angeles Reservoir. The plastic balls float on the water's surface, blocking sunlight and reducing the amount of water that evaporates. They reportedly will save 300 million gallons (1.1 billion L) of water, and they are relatively inexpensive compared to other conservation technology.[11] They will also help prevent algal blooms. Other drought technology included the development of fog mesh. This material collects water from low-hanging fog clouds. While the idea of collecting fog as it condenses on mesh seemed reasonable, the amount of mesh required to capture a gallon of water was very high. Approximately 20 square feet (2 sq m) would be needed to capture one gallon (3.8 L) of water in a day.[12] Officials also discussed the idea of trucking water in from wetter climates, but it would take tens of thousands of large shipments per day to meet demand.

those fields out of production as well. Similarly, cotton fields were switched over to different crops. By 2015, the production of cotton in California was approximately 10 percent of what it was in the 1980s.[13] If citizens, cities, and farmers applied all these methods of saving and reusing water, scientists estimate they could save 14 million acre-feet of water, enough to supply water to all the state's cities for a year.[14]

Vineyards, already prevalent in California, became even more widespread thanks to their relatively low water requirements.

DESALINATION

In order for seawater to be potable, it must be desalinated. The practice is not new. The ancient Greeks used primitive evaporation techniques to make drinkable water on sailing ships as early as the 300s BCE. When water evaporates, it separates from the salt. Once the evaporated water condenses, it can be collected and consumed.

In the 2000s, approximately 120 nations rely on desalination plants to convert large quantities of seawater to freshwater.[15] To start, ocean water is drawn into the plant via intake pipes covered with screens to keep marine life and other debris out. The water is then filtered and cleaned through a process called reverse osmosis. In this process, water is pushed through thousands of small tubes with semipermeable membranes. These layers allow water through but not other materials, such as salt particles. The freshwater that remains is pumped to aqueducts and reservoirs to meet water needs.

A desalination plant in Carlsbad, California, uses 2,000 individual tubes to turn salt water into freshwater. It can process 50 million gallons (189 million L) per day.

Chapter
NINE

INTO THE FUTURE

Prior to the winter of 2015–2016, experts predicted that it would take several years of above-average rainfall and good snowpack to lift California out of its drought. The likelihood of California receiving so much extra rain was low, but optimism ran high at the beginning of the winter. A weather phenomenon known as El Niño, which historically brings storms and rain to the state, was in effect. By the summer of 2016, the impact of California's drought had eased somewhat thanks to the El Niño conditions. But experts warned that while the outlook in the short run may

Dry conditions are likely to persist into the future across California.

be optimistic, the possibility that drought is the new normal is very real. Californians may need to further adapt to their dry climate.

SUSTAINABLE WATER

In May 2016, Governor Brown made some of the emergency water cuts permanent in an effort to make conservation a part of Californians' everyday lives. He also required urban areas to submit regular reports concerning water usage, conservation efforts, and enforcement practices. Nonetheless, some of the strict efficiency guidelines were dropped in some areas, renewing disputes over water allocation.

"Among all our uncertainties, weather is one of the most basic. We can't control it. We can only live with it, and now we have to live with a very serious drought of uncertain duration."[1]

—Governor Jerry Brown

Farmers will play important roles in shaping the future of water usage in California.

DROUGHT-FRIENDLY RECIPES

At the height of the California drought, when individuals were urged to make water conservation a priority, Nathan Lyon and Sarah Forman were inspired to design water-conscious recipes. They shopped for ingredients that require less water to produce than other foods and little water to cook. They also investigated ways to eliminate food waste. Then they created recipes with a small water footprint and a lot of flavor. The dishes tend to favor fruits, vegetables, and fish over beef. Lyon and Forman's intention was to make recipes that were both simple and delicious. The recipes would also make people think about the resources needed to bring a meal to the table.

The Metropolitan Water District of Southern California, overseeing a part of the state with drought conditions rated as extreme or exceptional, promptly did away with overuse fees and stiff rationing after the El Niño winter. The agency defended this move because supply had improved in the northern part of the state, where much of its water originates. The concern, however, was that residents would believe the drought was coming to an end rather than temporarily easing.

Leaders have yet to come to an agreement on how to best manage surface water. The arguments continue over water allocation, as well as what infrastructure is needed to best manage the water there is. The status of water rights remains a key issue. "Everybody with senior water rights has a huge interest in keeping the system exactly the way it is, even if it means hurting other people—which it does," said Thomas Holyoke, a water-politics expert from California State University, Fresno.[2] All the farmers, cities, and water agencies with senior water rights want to keep the system in place because it benefits them the most. These sectors have defended their rights in court.

By 2016, the debate was continuing over how to handle the situation. Many experts agreed more oversight of the water-rights system was needed. Without such oversight, it is difficult to know how much water there really is, how much is being used, where it is being used, and who is using it. The system is open to corruption and illegal use. Water experts believe the government needs to take control of the situation and require water-rights holders to report water use more regularly. Many also believe the state water board should have more power to enforce rights and usage.

BROADER WATER ISSUES

While attention has focused on California, drought is a reality facing much of the American West. Experts predict continued reductions in rainfall and increases in temperature. The water in the West is often over-allocated, and waterways such as the Colorado River are significantly emptier than they were in the past.

WASHING WITH AIR
The task of conserving water in California became everyone's responsibility, sparking some creative solutions. In one restaurant in the Big Sur region, the drought forced a chef to consider how much water went into washing dishes. With an air compressor already installed at the restaurant to help clean the stoves, he wondered if it could be converted to use at the sinks to prewash the dishes. Once the system was in place, the restaurant started saving an average of 1,000 gallons (3,800 L) of water per day.[4]

Beyond California, experts predict a global water crisis in the coming decades due to increased population and water misuse, mismanagement, and pollution. As of 2016, one billion people across the globe did not have access to clean, safe water.[3] Experts predict that number will increase as water becomes more scarce. This could have social and political implications, threatening stability in much of the world as people struggle for water sources.

Preserving California's scarce water resources for future generations will require a concerted effort by the government, corporations, and citizens.

THE FUTURE OF WATER

In order to meet water demands in California and globally, leaders must take a wide-ranging approach. No amount of engineering and infrastructure can completely solve water supply issues. Conservation by itself will not be enough, nor will the reallocation of water and water rights. People must address all these aspects of the water issue simultaneously.

Additionally, people will need to change the way they think about and manage water. Efficiency standards may need to be permanent rather than used only during droughts. California must overcome the political impasse over water rights, finding new compromises to satisfy the players involved. As the state comes to terms with the effects of climate change and extended drought, it is making moves toward a more sustainable water future.

WATER FOOTPRINTS

Every living organism on Earth has a water footprint based on how much water it utilizes. For humans, the water footprint is large because they not only consume water for hydration, but they also use it for cooking, bathing, cleaning, recreation, and more. Further, all manufactured goods, including food, require water for production. The production, consumption, and water usage choices each individual makes determine the size of his or her water footprint. As water issues become more pressing in a world with a growing population, scientists look at water footprints to better understand water consumption and make informed decisions for a sustainable water future. Understanding consumption on an individual level can also help people to be more conscious about their choices.

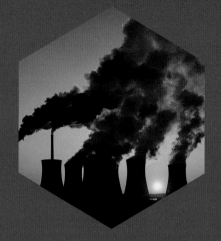

Climate Factors

Low precipitation
Less snowpack
Higher temperatures

Low reservoirs
Reduced surface water flows

Human Influence

Develop water infrastructure
Put water rights in place
Over-allocate water

Increased demand

Loss of income   Loss of jobs   Increased groundwater pumping   Aquifer depletion

Reduced water supply

Reduced agricultural production

Loss of hydropower

Human health risks

Risks to habitats

Fish and wildlife stressed

Trees and vegetation stressed

Species endangered

More frequent and intense fires

ESSENTIAL FACTS

WHAT IS HAPPENING

Beginning in 2012, California entered a prolonged drought period with less precipitation and higher-than-average temperatures. While California has a climate history that includes drought cycles, the latest one was said to be one of the worst in 1,200 years, and it was worsened by record-high temperatures across the state. Despite the massive water infrastructure in the state, including dams, reservoirs, and aqueducts, there was not enough water to meet demand in urban areas, agriculture, and the environment. By 2014, conditions had worsened and the state's governor, Jerry Brown, declared a drought state of emergency.

THE CAUSES

The natural causes of the drought combined with human factors that impacted water supplies. A complicated set of water laws mandate who in the state gets water, how much, and when, and has little government oversight. In addition, water has been over-allocated in California for decades, meaning some sectors have rights to more water than there actually is, especially in drought years. Populations have continued to grow dramatically in California as well, putting additional strain on the water supply.

KEY PLAYERS

» California governor Jerry Brown called for reduced water consumption to ease the effects of the drought. He allocated funds for emergency relief and assistance to individuals and also for education, conservation, and water projects.

» The agricultural industry, which uses much of the state's water, was hit especially hard by the drought. Some farmers turned to groundwater pumping to save their crops.

» Ordinary California citizens have been affected by the drought. Some in rural areas saw their wells run completely dry and required water support from the government. All over the state, people had to conserve water and rethink how they used it.

WHAT IT MEANS FOR THE FUTURE

California's drought is likely to have long-term effects on the lifestyle of Californians as water conservation measures become the new normal. The suffering of the environment and wildlife from the drought conditions seems likely to continue. Groundwater pumping increased so dramatically during the drought that experts warned the aquifers were being permanently depleted. The pumping also led to dramatic subsidence, and some areas experienced severe cases of land sinking. The lack of moisture will also continue to make wildfires more severe.

QUOTE

"People should realize we are in a new era. The idea of your nice little green lawn getting watered every day, those days are past."

—*California governor Jerry Brown, 2015*

GLOSSARY

acre-foot

The amount of water it takes to fill an area the size of an acre (0.405 ha) to one foot (30.5 cm) of depth. One acre-foot is equal to 325,851 gallons (1,233,480 L).

aqueduct

A pipe or channel built to carry water over a long distance.

climate

The average weather in a region over a period of years.

commodity

Something that has value and is bought and sold.

desalination

The process by which salt and minerals are removed from salty water.

estuary

An area where river water meets seawater.

evapotranspiration

A loss of moisture into the atmosphere through evaporation and transpiration.

fallow

Left untilled and unused.

firebreak

A space cleared of flammable plants, intended to block the spread of a fire.

gray water

Water from showers, bathtubs, washing machines, sinks, and kitchens that can be collected to use again.

paleoclimatology

The science dealing with the climate of past ages.

potable

Safe to drink.

snowpack

The accumulation of packed snow over a season.

subsidence

The gradual caving in or sinking of an area of land.

subsidy

Money paid, usually by a government, to keep the price of a product or service low.

unsustainable

Not able to continue at a current rate or level.

ADDITIONAL RESOURCES

SELECTED BIBLIOGRAPHY

"California Water Science Center." *US Geological Survey*. US Geological Survey, n.d. Web. 14 Sept. 2016.

Carle, David. *Water and the California Dream: Historic Choices for Shaping the Future*. Berkeley, CA: Counterpoint, 2016. Print.

Lassiter, Allison. *Sustainable Water—Challenges and Solutions from California*. Oakland, CA: U of California P, 2015. Print.

FURTHER READINGS

Carle, David. *Introduction to Water in California*. Oakland: U of California P, 2016. Print.

Flood, Nancy Bo. *Water Runs through This Book*. Golden, CO: Fulcrum, 2015. Print.

Leahy, Stephen. *Your Water Footprint: The Shocking Facts about How Much Water We Use to Make Everyday Products*. Buffalo, NY: Firefly, 2014. Print.

WEBSITES

To learn more about Ecological Disasters, visit **abdobooklinks.com**. These links are routinely monitored and updated to provide the most current information available.

FOR MORE INFORMATION

For more information on this subject, contact or visit the following organizations:

Carlsbad Desalination Plant

5780 Fleet Street
Carlsbad, CA 92008
760-655-3900
http://carlsbaddesal.com

This desalination plant takes ocean water and makes it potable, delivering quality, safe, drought-proof drinking water to the residents of San Diego County.

National Drought Mitigation Center

University of Nebraska–Lincoln
819 Hardin Hall
3310 Holdrege Street, PO Box 830988
Lincoln, NE 68583–0988
402-472-6707
http://drought.unl.edu

Since 1995, the National Drought Mitigation Center has assisted the public in understanding human vulnerability to drought and developed risk management strategies.

SOURCE NOTES

CHAPTER 1. EXTREME DROUGHT

1. Kerry Klein and Sasha Khokha. "Hundreds of Millions in Drought Relief Failing to Reach Many Californians." *Community Water Center*. Community Water Center, 19 Sept. 2015. Web. 16 Sept. 2016.

2. Ibid.

3. Scott Smith. "When the Wells Run Dry: California Neighbors Cope in Drought." *Cnsnews.com*. Media Research Center, 1 Sept. 2015. Web. 13 Sept. 2016.

4. Ibid.

5. Ezra Romero. "As Wells Dry Up, Calif. County Aims to Streamline Solutions for Water." *NPR*. NPR, 26 May 2015. Web. 20 Sept. 2016.

6. "Types of Drought." *National Drought Mitigation Center*. University of Nebraska–Lincoln, n.d. Web. 16 Sept. 2016.

7. Ian Lovett. "California Braces for Unending Drought." *New York Times*. New York Times Company, 9 May 2016. Web. 20 Sept. 2016.

8. "Breaking News—East Porterville Homes Connected to Water System; Pipes Deliver Relief to Residents in Drought's 'Ground Zero.'" *California Department of Water Resources*. State of California, n.d. Web. 20 Sept. 2016.

CHAPTER 2. DROUGHT IN CONTEXT

1. Daniel Griffin and Kevin J. Anchukaitis. "How Unusual Is the 2012–2014 Drought?" *Geophysical Research Letters*. AGU Publications, 28 Dec. 2014 Web. 22 Sept. 2016.

2. Preston Fitzgerald, ed. *California's Water Concerns*. New York: Nova, 2015. Print. 44.

3. Ibid.

4. "California Temperatures on the Rise." *Earth Observatory*. NASA, 17 Apr. 2007. Web. 3 Oct. 2016.

5. Rich Pedroncelli. "A Guide to California's Drought and Water Crisis." *Sacramento Bee*. Sacramento Bee, 28 May 2015. Web. 11 Oct. 2016.

6. Tom Di Liberto. "How Deep of a Precipitation Hole Is California In?" *Climate.gov*. NOAA, 11 Sept. 2015. Web. 3 Oct. 2016.

7. "Climate of California." *Regional Western Climate Center*. Regional Western Climate Center, n.d. Web. 11 Oct. 2016.

8. Brian Clark Howard. "Snowpack 97% of Average in California's Northern Sierra." *National Geographic*. National Geographic Society, 30 Mar. 2016. Web. 3 Oct. 2016.

9. Amanda Zamora, Lauren Kirchner, and Abrahm Lustgarten. "California's Drought Is Part of a Much Bigger Water Crisis. Here's What You Need to Know." *Pro Publica*. Pro Publica, 25 June 2015. Web. 3 Oct. 2016.

10. "California Climate Strategy." *California Climate Change*. State of California, n.d. Web. 27 Sept. 2016.

CHAPTER 3. THE HUMAN FACTOR

1. Nathanael Johnson. "Everything I Thought I Knew about Water in California Is Wrong." *Grist*. Grist Magazine, 20 Apr. 2015. Web. 3 Oct. 2016.

2. Kevin Oliver. "Folsom Lake Dry Spell Reveals Submerged Gold Rush Town." *KCRA3*. KCRA-TV, 18 Jan. 2014. Web. 1 Oct. 2016.

3. Adam Nagourney, Jack Healy, and Nelson D. Schwartz. "California Drought Tests History of Endless Growth." *New York Times*. New York Times Company, 4 Apr. 2015. Web. 1 Oct. 2016.

4. "Los Angeles Aqueduct." *History Channel*. History Channel, n.d. Web. 25 Jan. 2017.

5. Bryan Walsh. "Hundred Years of Dry: How California's Drought Could Get Much, Much Worse." *TIME*. TIME, 23 Jan. 2014. Web. 22 Sept. 2016.

6. Brian Clark Howard. "California Drought Launches New Gold Rush." *National Geographic*. National Geographic Society, 15 Aug. 2014. Web. 12 Oct. 2016.

7. Abrahm Lustgarten, David Sleight, Amanda Zamora, Lauren Kirchner, and John Grimwade. "What You Need to Know about the Water Crisis in the West." *Pro Publica*. Pro Publica, 27 May 2015. Web. 11 Oct. 2016.

8. Steve Scauzillo. "Drought Is Killing California's Hydroelectric Power. Can Solar Make Up the Difference?" *CAdrought.com*. California Newspaper Partnership, 16 Sept. 2015. Web. 12 Oct. 2016.

9. "Hydroelectric Power in California." *California Energy Commission*. State of California, n.d. Web. 12 Oct. 2016.

10. "California Drought Leads to Less Hydropower, Increased Natural Gas Generation." *US Energy Information Administration*. US Department of Energy, 6 Oct. 2014. Web. 12 Oct. 2016.

CHAPTER 4. THE URBAN SECTOR

1. "Governor's Drought Declaration." *California Department of Water Resources*. State of California, n.d. Web. 16 Sept. 2016.

2. Melissa S. Kearney, Benjamin H. Harris, Brad Hershbein, Elisa Jácome, and Gregory Nantz. "In Times of Drought: Nine Economic Facts about Water in the United States." *Hamilton Project*. Hamilton Project, 14 Oct. 2014. Web. 25 Jan. 2017.

3. Adam Nagourney. "California Imposes First Mandatory Water Restrictions to Deal with Drought." *New York Times*. New York Times Company, 1 Apr. 2015. Web. 1 Oct. 2016.

4. Steve Scauzillo. "LA County Cemetery—Largest in Nation—Will Use 100 Percent Recycled Water." *CAdrought.com*. California Newspaper Partnership, 31 Aug. 2015. Web. 1 Oct. 2016.

5. Thomas Suh Lauder. "Look Up Drought Report Cards for California's Urban Water Districts." *Los Angeles Times*. Los Angeles Times, 6 May 2016. Web. 1 Oct. 2016.

6. Chris Garner. "Water-wise, Long Beach Setting a Good Example." *Save Our Water*. Association of California Water Agencies and the California Department of Water Resources, 19 Sept. 2016. Web. 1 Oct. 2016.

7. Luke Whelan. "The Drought Is Behind California's Skyrocketing West Nile Virus Numbers." *Mother Jones*. Mother Jones, 13 Apr. 2015. Web. 1 Oct. 2016.

8. Ezra David Romero. "Drought-Friendly Recipes Kick Up the Flavor—and Cut Back on Water." *Colorado Public Radio*. NPR, 8 June 2015. Web. 30 Sept. 2016.

9. "Best and Worst Foods in California's Drought." *WIRED*. Condé Nast, 4 June 2015. Web. 30 Sept. 2016.

CHAPTER 5. THE AGRICULTURAL SECTOR

1. David Carle. *Water and the California Dream–Historic Choices for Shaping the Future*. Berkeley, CA: Counterpoint, 2016. Print. 200.

2. Preston Fitzgerald, ed. *California's Water Concerns*. New York: Nova, 2015. Print. 41.

3. Nathanael Johnson. "Everything I Thought I Knew about Water in California Is Wrong." *Grist*. Grist Magazine, 20 Apr. 2015. Web. 3 Oct. 2016.

4. Carrie Halperin and Sean Patrick Farrell, producers. "California's Extreme Drought, Explained." *YouTube*. YouTube, 7 July 2014. Web. 3 Oct. 2016.

5. Hannah Yi. "See How a Historic Drought Has Changed California's Landscape." *PBS News Hour*. NewsHour Productions, 13 Dec. 2014. Web. 3 Oct. 2016.

6. Ibid.

7. Andrea Castillo. "How Drought Has Hit Farmworkers Hard in Fresno, Tulare Counties." *Fresno Bee*. Fresno Bee, 4 Dec. 2015. Web. 3 Oct. 2016.

8. Mareesa Nicosia. "The Forgotten Students of California's Drought." *Atlantic*. Atlantic Monthly Group, 10 Sept. 2015. Web. 1 Oct. 2016.

9. "California's Drought Ripples through Businesses, Then to Schools." *Colorado Public Radio*. NPR, 20 Apr. 2014. Web. 3 Oct. 2016.

10. Carrie Halperin and Sean Patrick Farrell, producers. "California's Extreme Drought, Explained." *YouTube*. YouTube, 7 July 2014. Web. 3 Oct. 2016.

11. Richard Gonzales. "How Almonds Became a Scapegoat for California's Drought." *Colorado Public Radio*. NPR, 16 Apr. 2015. Web. 3 Oct. 2016.

12. Hannah Yi. "See How a Historic Drought Has Changed California's Landscape." *PBS News Hour*. NewsHour Productions, 13 Dec. 2014. Web. 3 Oct. 2016.

13. Jeff Daniels. "California Drought Costs to Top $600 Million." *CNBC*. CNBC, 15 Aug. 2016. Web. 15 Oct. 2016.

CHAPTER 6. THE ENVIRONMENT

1. Natalya Estrada. "Feds, Tribes React to Trinity Water Releases." *Times Standard News*. Eureka Times-Standard, 25 Aug. 2016. Web. 15 Oct. 2016.

2. Bettina Boxall. "The Drought's Hidden Victim: California's Native Fish." *Los Angeles Times*. Los Angeles Times, 24 Aug. 2015. Web. 5 Oct. 2016.

3. "What If California's Drought Continues?" *Public Policy Institute of California*. PPIC, Aug. 2015. Web. 25 Jan. 2017.

4. Kirk Siegler. "Endangered Species Protections at Center of Drought Debate." *Colorado Public Radio*. NPR, 15 June 2015. Web. 15 Oct. 2016.

5. Bettina Boxall. "The Drought's Hidden Victim: California's Native Fish." *Los Angeles Times*. Los Angeles Times, 24 Aug. 2015. Web. 5 Oct. 2016.

6. Hannah Yi. "See How a Historic Drought Has Changed California's Landscape." *PBS News Hour*. NewsHour Productions, 13 Dec. 2014. Web. 3 Oct. 2016.

7. Dennis Dimick. "If You Think the Water Crisis Can't Get Worse, Wait until the Aquifers Are Drained." *National Geographic*. National Geographic Society, 21 Aug. 2014. Web. 15 Oct. 2016.

8. Lisa M. Krieger. "California Drought: Parts of Central Valley Sinking 2 Inches a Month." *CAdrought.com*. California Newspaper Partnership, 25 Aug. 2015. Web. 15 Oct. 2016.

9. Amy Quinton. "Bees Feeling Effects of California Drought." *Capital Public Radio*. Capital Public Radio, 6 Mar. 2014. Web. 5 Oct. 2016.

10. "Migratory Birds Impacted by California Drought." *Al Jazeera America*. Al Jazeera America, 7 Nov. 2015. Web. 5 Oct. 2016.

11. Madison Kotack. "Even Indoor Kids Should Worry about California's 30 Million Dead Trees." *WIRED*. Condé Nast, 15 June 2016. Web. 6 Oct. 2016.

12. Eline Gordts. "Eleven Experts to Watch on California Water Rights." *News Deeply*. News Deeply, 9 Aug. 2016. Web. 15 Oct. 2016.

13. Becky Oskin. "Aquifers: Underground Stores of Freshwater." *Live Science*. Live Science, 14 Jan. 2015. Web. 15 Oct. 2015.

CHAPTER 7. WILDFIRES

1. Sammy Roth. "Record Temperatures Are Making Wildfire Season Worse." *Desert Sun*. Desert Sun, 14 Sept. 2016. Web. 5 Oct. 2016.

2. Paige St. John and Hailey Branson-Potts. "Man Arrested on Suspicion of Arson in Wildfire That Has Devastated Northern California Community." *Los Angeles Times*. Los Angeles Times, 15 Aug. 2016. Web. 7 Oct. 2016.

3. "Pilot Fire." *Incident Information System*. InciWeb, 16 Dec. 2016. Web. 25 Jan. 2017.

4. Sammy Roth. "Record Temperatures Are Making Wildfire Season Worse." *Desert Sun*. Desert Sun, 14 Sept. 2016. Web. 5 Oct. 2016.

5. Ibid.

6. "Emergency Fund Fire Suppression Expenditures." *Cal Fire*. State of California, Sept. 2014. Web. 25 Jan. 2017.

CHAPTER 8. LIVING WITH THE NEW NORMAL

1. Zain Haidar. "California Gov. Jerry Brown Announces $1 Billion Drought Plan." *Weather Channel*. Weather Channel, 20 Mar. 2015. Web. 15 Oct. 2015.

2. Spencer Millsap, producer. "How Innovative Tech Helps Fight California's Drought." *YouTube*. YouTube, 16 Oct. 2015. Web. 11 Oct. 2016.

3. Kirk Siegler. "Coping in a Drier World: California's Drought Survival Strategy." *Colorado Public Radio*. NPR, 22 Oct. 2014. Web. 15 Oct. 2015.

4. Ellen Knickmeyer and Kristen Gelineau. "California Looks to Australia for Drought Advice." *CAdrought.com*. California Newspaper Partnership, 10 June 2015. Web. 11 Oct. 2016.

5. Wayne Freedman. "North Bay Teen's Creative Fix for California Drought." *ABC 7 News*. ABC, 12 Sept. 2014. Web. 11 Oct. 2016.

6. Lisa M. Krieger "In the Arid Coachella Valley, Communities Are Taking a Hell-or-High-Water Approach to Growth." *CAdrought.com*. California Newspaper Partnership, 14 Oct. 2015. Web. 11 Oct. 2016.

7. Donna Little John. "Could Lake Water from Alaska Be Shipped to L.A., Long Beach Ports?" *CAdrought.com*. California Newspaper Partnership, 15 Oct. 2015. Web. 11 Oct. 2016.

8. "Is Desalination the Future of Drought Relief in California?" *YouTube*. YouTube, 31 Oct. 2015. Web. 15 Oct. 2016.

9. "Pure Water San Diego Program." *City of San Diego*. City of San Diego, Sept. 2016. Web. 15 Oct. 2016.

10. Kirk Siegler. "Coping in a Drier World: California's Drought Survival Strategy." *Colorado Public Radio*. NPR, 22 Oct. 2014. Web. 15 Oct. 2015.

11. Sophia Chen. "Let's Rate the Dumbest Solutions to California's Drought." *WIRED*. Condé Nast, 12 Aug. 2015. Web. 11 Oct. 2016.

12. Ibid.

13. Lesley McClurg. "Squeezed by Drought, California Farmers Switch to Less Thirsty Crops." *Colorado Public Radio*. NPR, 28 July 2015. Web. 15 Oct. 2016.

14. Katherine Noyes. "Can Technology Help Us Survive California's Drought?" *Fortune*. Fortune Magazine, 11 Aug. 2014. Web. 15 Oct. 2016.

15. "Is Desalination the Future of Drought Relief in California?" *YouTube*. YouTube, 31 Oct. 2015. Web. 15 Oct. 2016.

CHAPTER 9. INTO THE FUTURE

1. Bryan Walsh. "Hundred Years of Dry: How California's Drought Could Get Much, Much Worse." *TIME*. TIME, 23 Jan. 2014. Web. 22 Sept. 2016.

2. Sammy Roth. "Record Temperatures Are Making Wildfire Season Worse." *Desert Sun*. Desert Sun, 14 Sept. 2016. Web. 5 Oct. 2016.

3. "Water Scarcity and the Importance of Water." *Water Project*. Water Project, n.d. Web. 15 Oct. 2016.

4. Angela Matano. "Trying to Conserve Water? Here's How to Pre-rinse Dishes with Air." *Los Angeles Times*. Los Angeles Times, 12 June 2015. Web. 15 Oct. 2016.

INDEX

ABOUT THE AUTHOR

Laura Perdew is an author, writing consultant, and former middle school teacher. She writes fiction and nonfiction for children, including numerous titles for the education market. She is also the author of *Kids on the Move! Colorado*, a guide to traveling through Colorado with children. Perdew lives and plays in Boulder with her husband and twin boys.